CW00409321

Christmas
Spirituals
for Choirs

12 specially commissioned
choral arrangements

Compiled and edited by

Bob Chilcott * Ken Burton

MUSIC DEPARTMENT

OXFORD
UNIVERSITY PRESS

OXFORD
UNIVERSITY PRESS

Great Clarendon Street, Oxford OX2 6DP, England
198 Madison Avenue, New York, NY10016, USA

Oxford is a registered trade mark of Oxford University Press
in the UK and in certain other countries

Christmas Spirituals *for* Choirs

Christmas is a time of year when singing comes into its own, helping us to
express a communal joy both in sacred and secular contexts. It is also the
season when choral singers are keen to explore new music alongside more
traditional works.

In this collection of 12 specially commissioned pieces, the contributors have
embraced the spiritual form with this in mind. Here you will discover
traditional spirituals in new arrangements, and new pieces inspired by well-
known and less familiar Christmas texts.

In forming this collection, Ken Burton, Bob Chilcott, and Roderick
Williams have drawn upon an amazing wealth of musical experiences.
Their hope is that *Christmas Spirituals* will succeed in narrating the
Christmas story with music of the highest quality, and will inspire joy
through singing at this most beautiful time of the year.

CONTENTS

1. And His name shall be called

Words and music by
KEN BURTON

OXFORD UNIVERSITY PRESS, MUSIC DEPARTMENT, GREAT CLARENDON STREET, OXFORD OX2 6DP

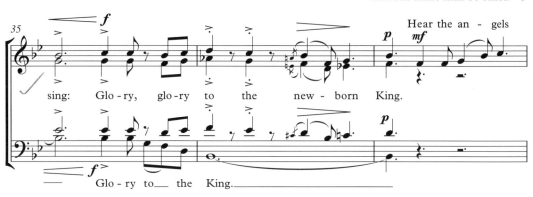

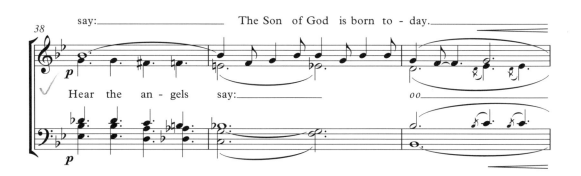

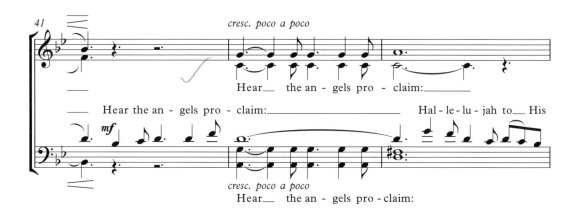

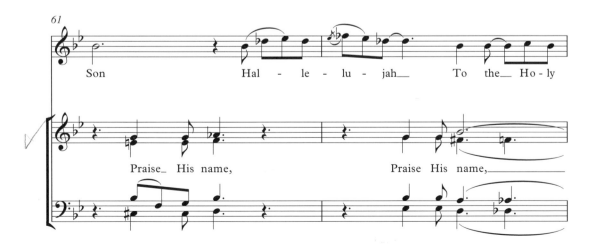

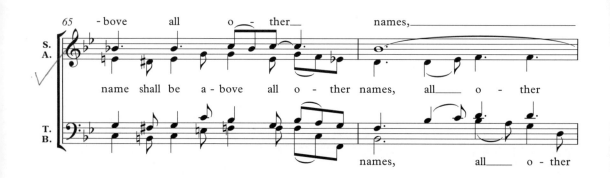

for Fern and Heather

2. Away in a manger

Words anon.
(19th cent. American)

Melody by W. J. KIRKPATRICK
(1838–1921)
arr. BOB CHILCOTT

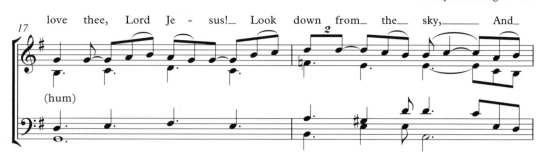

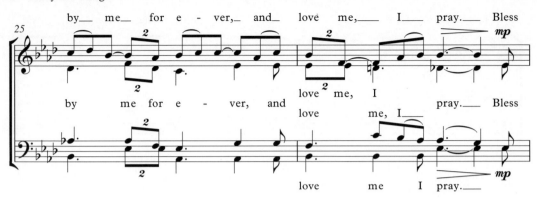

for Steve Jones and the City Chamber Choir

3. Behold that star

arr. BOB CHILCOTT

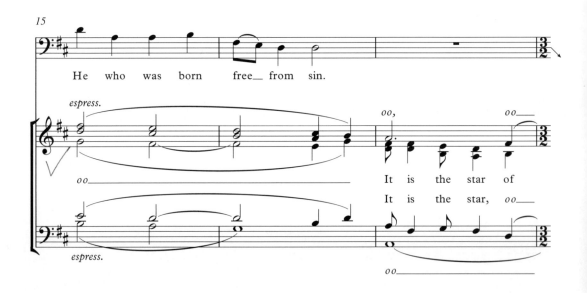

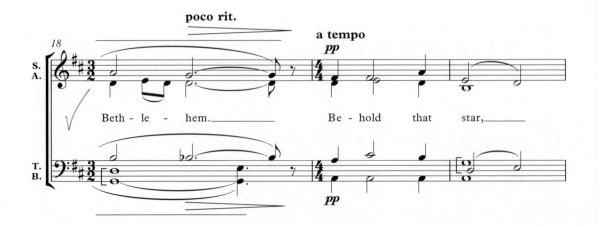

Be - hold that star up yon - der, Be - hold that

star,____ It is the star of Beth - le - hem,__ oh

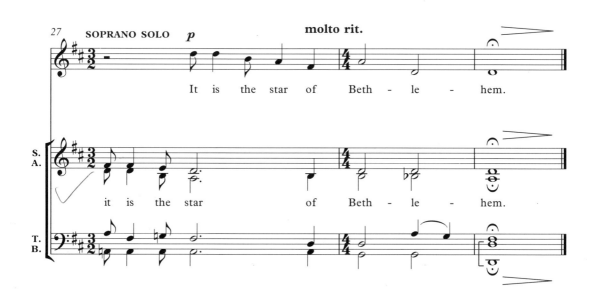

SOPRANO SOLO *p*   molto rit.

It is the star of Beth - le - hem.

it is the star of Beth - le - hem.

4. Children, go where I send thee

arr. RODERICK WILLIAMS

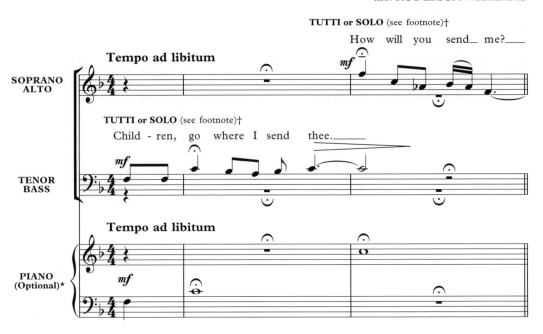

* It may be desirable to have the bass line played on another instrument (electric bass) or even to have two players at the keyboard, dividing bass line and harmony ad lib.

† These ad lib. bars (see also bars 83, 84, and 102) can be solo, with complete freedom, or tutti as notated.

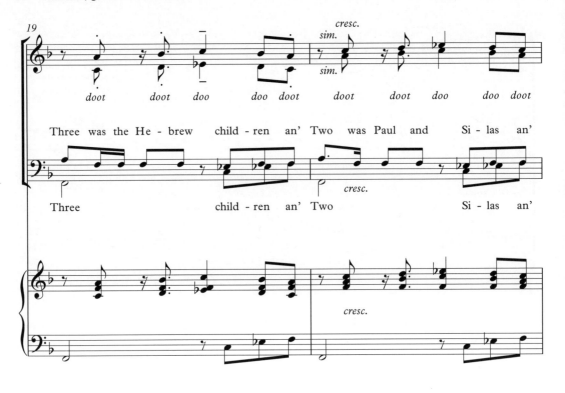

* Ideally the l.h. should shadow the bass vocal part. If this becomes too
complicated against the rhythm in the r.h., a simplified version can be used:

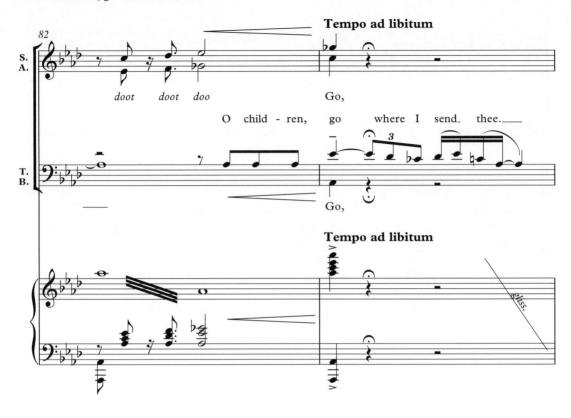

* From this point onwards a crossed notehead ✗ indicates that a word is to be spoken not sung.

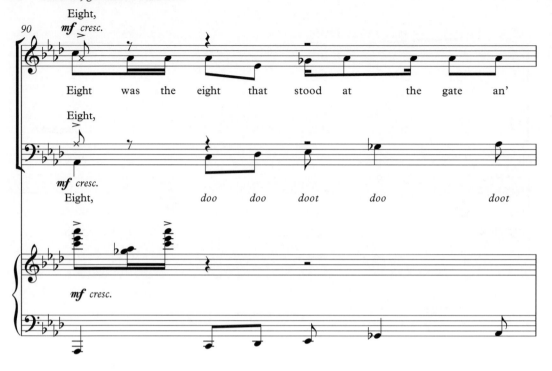

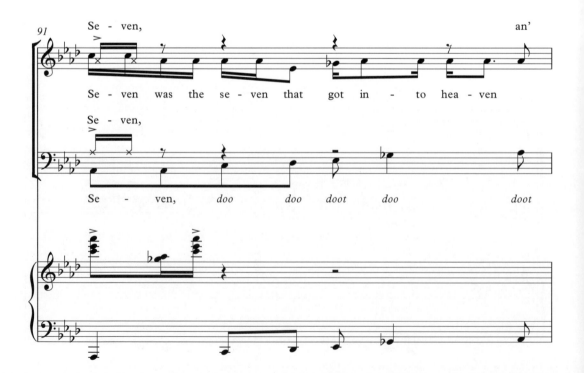

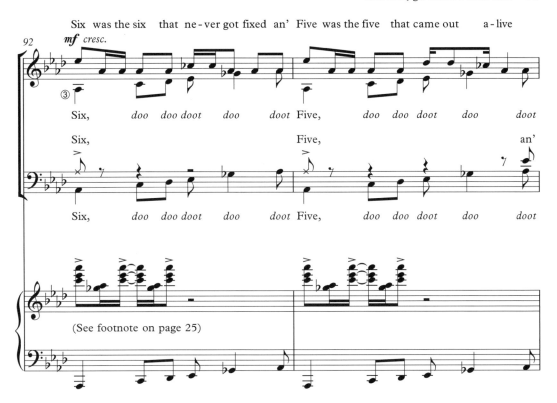

Two   was Paul an'   Si - las   an'   One   was the lid - dle bid - dy   ba - by that's

Two,   *doo doo doot doo*   *doot*   One,   *doo*   *doo*   *doot doo*   *doot*

Subito meno mosso 'bluesy'

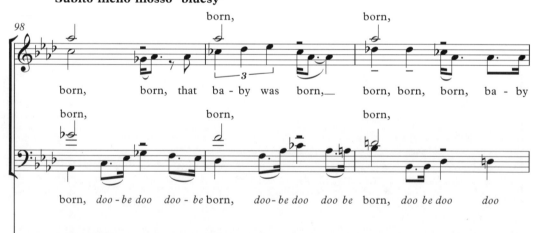

born,   born,

born,   born,   that   ba - by   was   born,___   born,   born,   born,   ba - by

born,   born,   born,

born,   *doo - be doo*   *doo - be* born,   *doo - be doo   doo be* born,   *doo be doo*   *doo*

Subito meno mosso 'bluesy'

① (p.30) The vocal bass line can be developed ad lib. using extra percussive sounds with the piano shadowing (see footnote page 25); this *ossia* is an example:

I, *doo doo doot doo - ba doot*

② (p.34) The bass line can be further developed ad lib:

I, *t k dum dum bum t bum ti bum*

③ (p.37) The alto and soprano parts should copy whatever bass pattern is used in bar 85.

Six, *t k dum dum bum t bum ti bum*

Four, *t k dum dum bum t bum ti bum*

5. Go, tell it on the mountain

arr. KEN BURTON

In hummed passages repeated notes should be articulated.

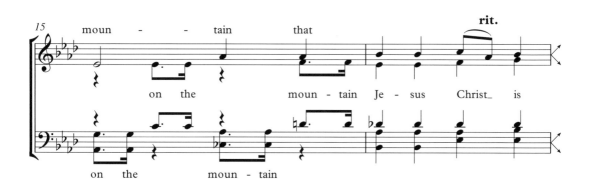

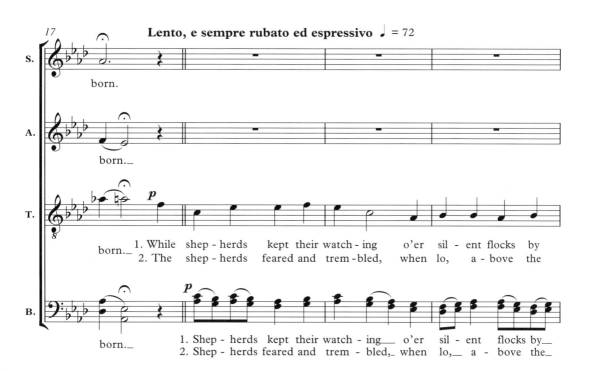

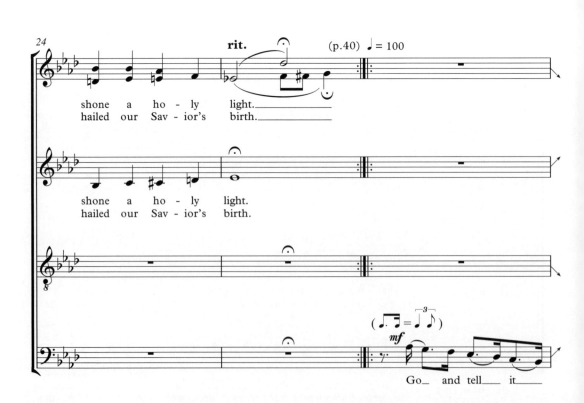

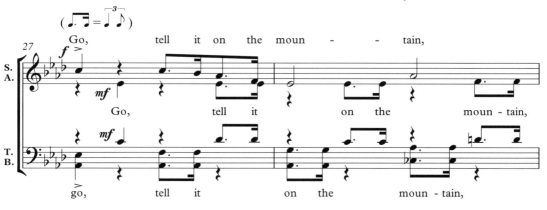

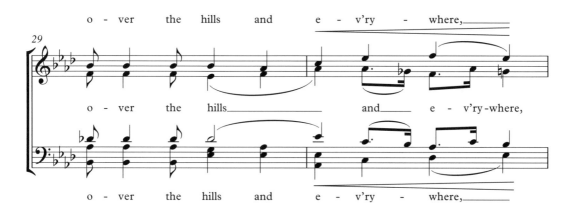

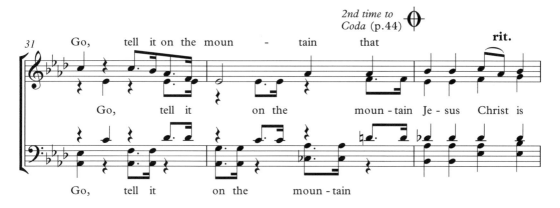

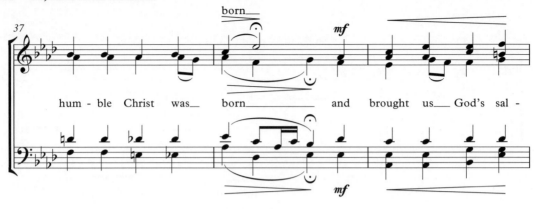

hum - ble Christ was__ born_____ and   brought us__ God's sal -

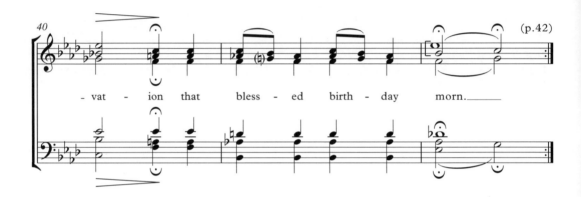

(p.42)

- vat - ion that bless - ed birth - day morn.__

CODA

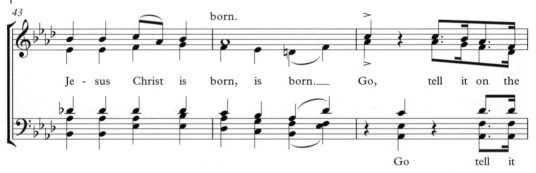

Je - sus Christ is born, is born.__   Go,   tell it on the

Go   tell it

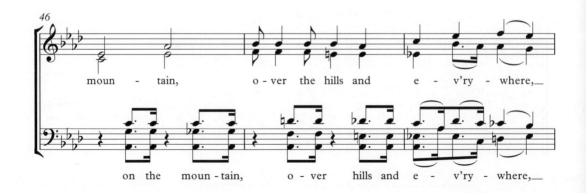

moun - tain,   o - ver the hills and   e - v'ry - where,__

on the moun - tain,   o - ver hills and e - v'ry - where,__

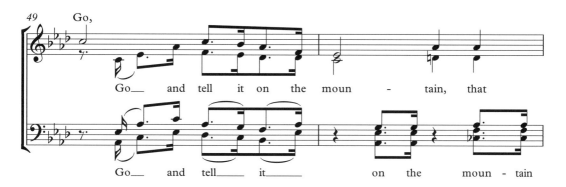

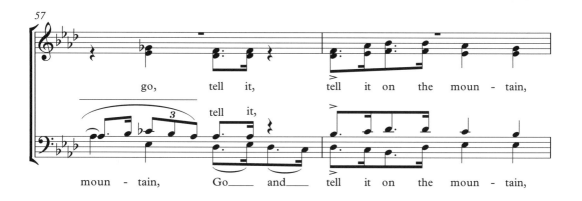

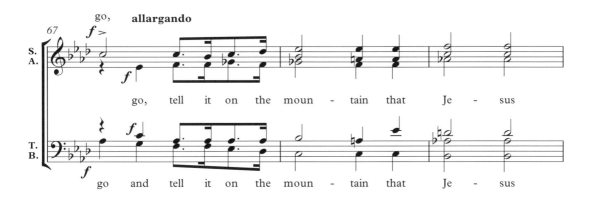

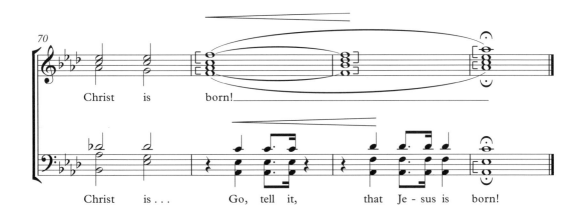

6. Mary had a baby

arr. RODERICK WILLIAMS

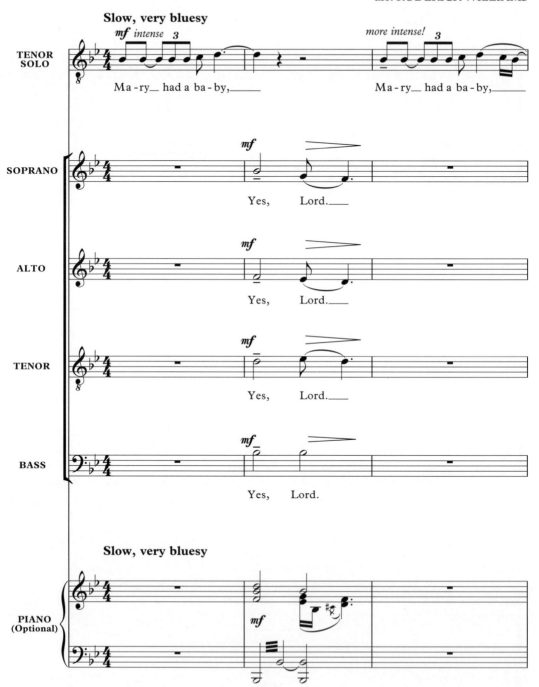

* Solo part can join chorus line here ad lib.

* Falsetto ad lib.

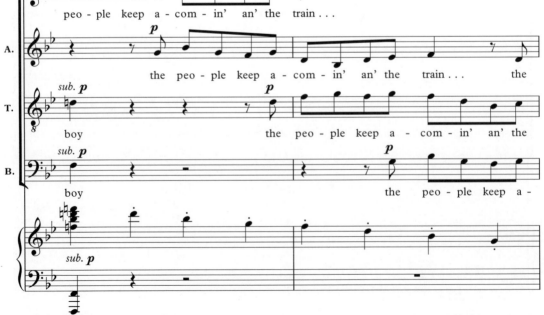

* Solo part can join chorus line here ad lib.

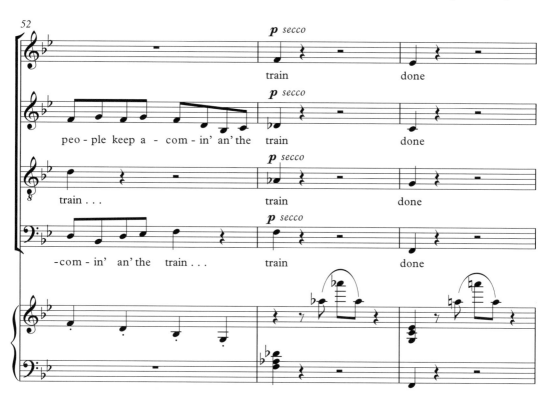

for Ken Burton and the London Adventist Chorale

7. Mighty Wonder

St Germanus (634– *c.*733)
tr. J. M. Neale (1818–1866)

Music by
BOB CHILCOTT

with ho - nour

The Vir - gin bears the In - fant with vir - gin ho - nour pure. Re-

pure. Re - peat the hymn a - gain: 'To

- peat the hymn a - gain: 'To

God on high_ be glo - ry, to God on high_ be glo - ry,_ and

peace on__ earth_____ to__ men!'

earth, peace on earth

'To God on high be glo - ry, to God on high be
God on high_ be glo - ry, to God on high_ be glo - ry,_ and

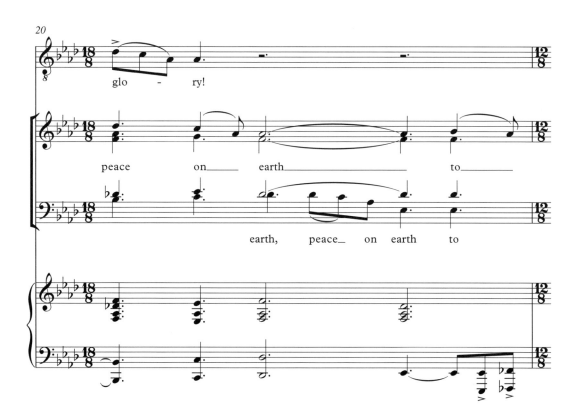

glo - ry!
peace on_ earth_ to_
earth, peace_ on earth to

Since all he comes to ran-som, By all__ he is a-dored,__ The

__ The In - fant born in Beth - le - hem,

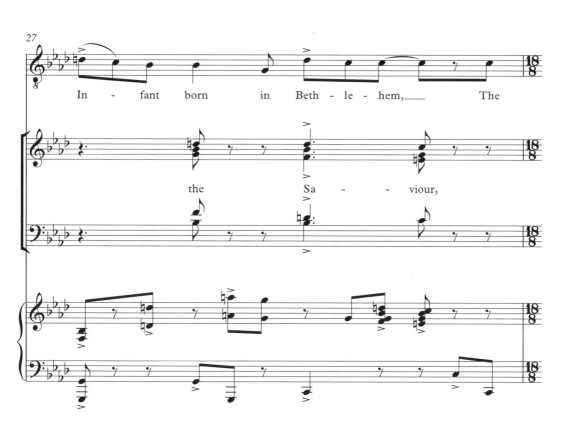

In - fant born in Beth - le - hem,__ The

the Sa - - viour,

Sa-viour, the Sa - - viour and the Lord.

the Sa-viour and_____ the Lord.

oo_____ migh - ty

oo_____

S.
A.

T.
B.

While thus they sing your Mo-narch,

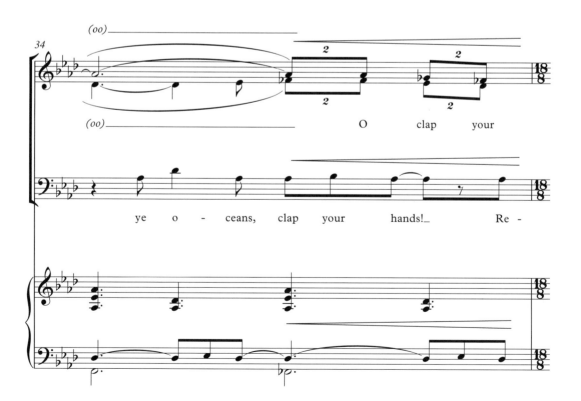

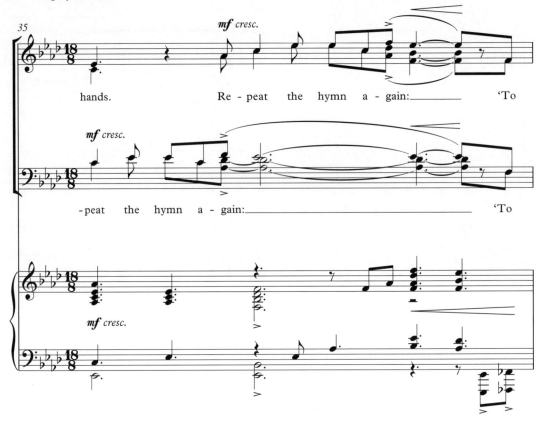

hands.   Re - peat   the   hymn   a - gain:_____   'To

-peat   the   hymn   a - gain:_____ 'To

God on high_ be glo - ry,   to   God on high_ be glo - ry,____ and

for Gillian Dibden and the Berkshire Youth Choir

8. Remember, O thou man

Thomas Ravenscroft?
(*c.*1582–1635)

Music by
BOB CHILCOTT

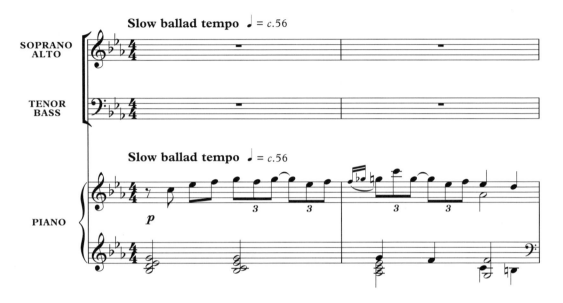

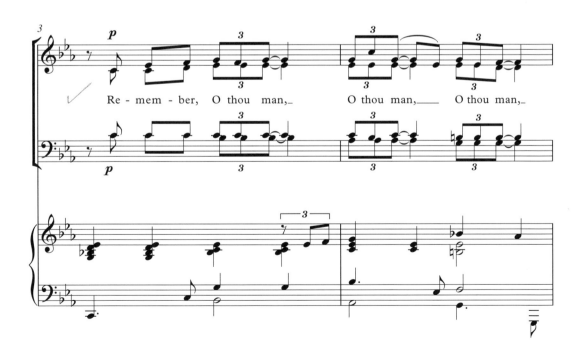

On heav'ns high hill!___ The an - gels all did sing__

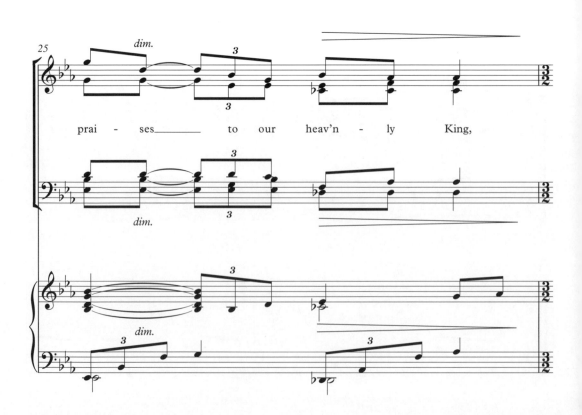

prai - ses___ to our heav'n - ly King,

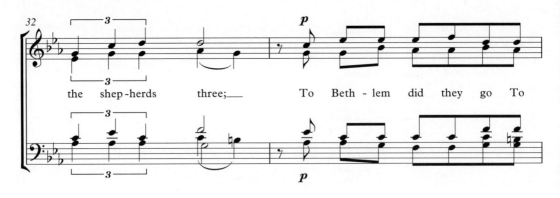

the shep-herds   three;___   To Beth - lem did they go To

see whe-ther   it were so,___   whe-ther Christ was born or no__ to set man

S.
A.

free,_____   to set man   free.___

T.
B.

Pno

to Albrecht Schneider and the Landesjugendchor Rheinland-Pfalz

9. Rise up, shepherd, and follow

arr. BOB CHILCOTT

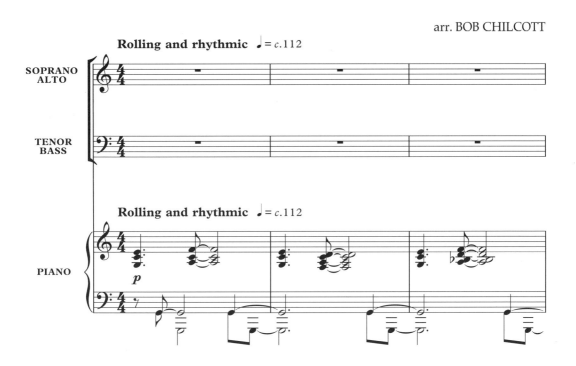

There's a star in the east on Christ-mas morn,

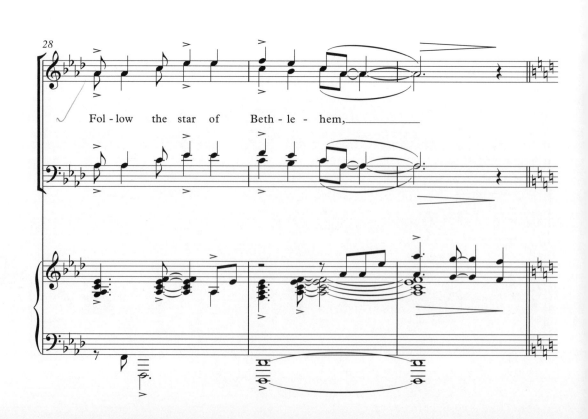

Rise_ up, shep - herd,_____ fol - low.___

and   fol - low,   fol - low._____

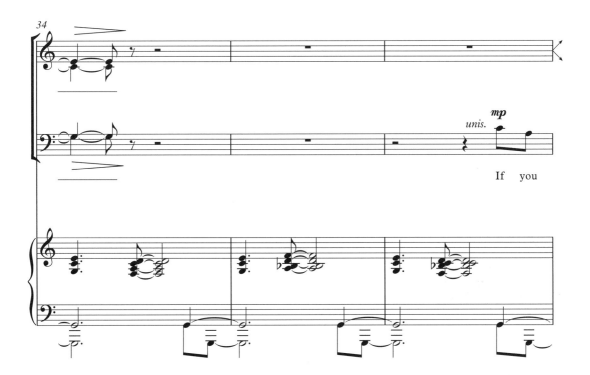

If   you

Rise up, shep-herd and fol - low;___ Fol-low the star of

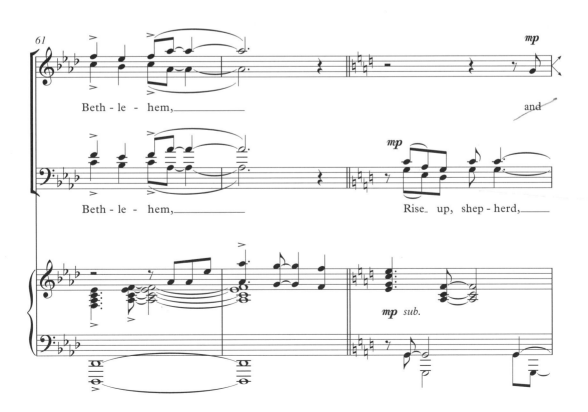

Beth - le - hem,___

Beth - le - hem,___   Rise_ up, shep - herd,___   and

10. Star of the night

Words and music by
KEN BURTON

Notes

1. Where the choir is singing 'oos', 'ahs', or 'hms', there are occasions where several notes
   in succession of the same pitch have been written over the one syllable (e.g. bar 1 has the
   rhythm ♪♩ written over the first 2 Ds). The choir should treat these as tied notes, but
   articulate the rhythm as written. The best way to do this is to place an acciacatura before
   the repeated note, or treat it in the same way as a string player using up-bows and down-bows.

2. The choir can do humming instead of 'oos' if preferred.

3. The solos are intended for three different males, to represent the traditional image of
   three wise men. However, it can be done by one, two or even more (the Bible does not
   record how many there were, simply stating 'wise men').

earth, for us to die.
oo oo oo
molto espress.
oo oo oo
molto espress.

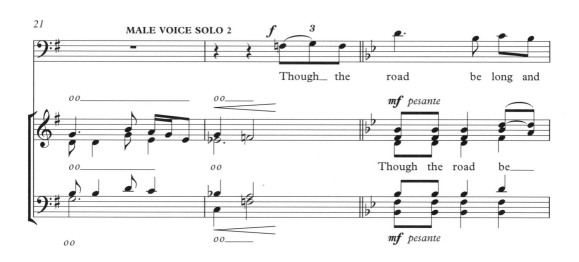

MALE VOICE SOLO 2 *f*
Though the road be long and
oo oo
oo oo
mf pesante
Though the road be
mf pesante

wear-y, The rains may fall, and winds may blow. The star still
long and wea-ry Rains may fall and winds may blow
blow.
long and wea-ry Rains may fall and winds may blow.

* Keyboard reduction. For rehearsal only.

49

52

meno mosso

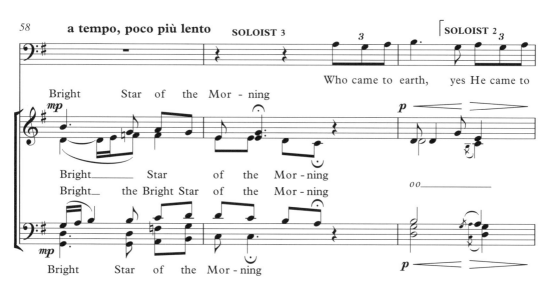

11. The Virgin Mary had a baby boy

West Indian
arr. KEN BURTON

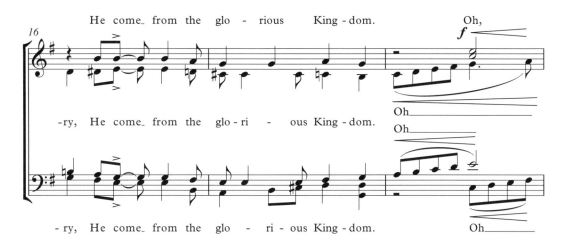

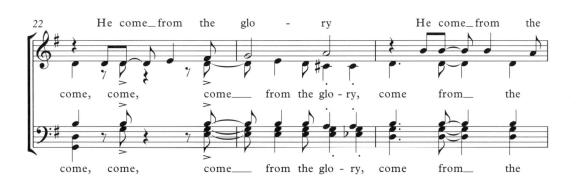

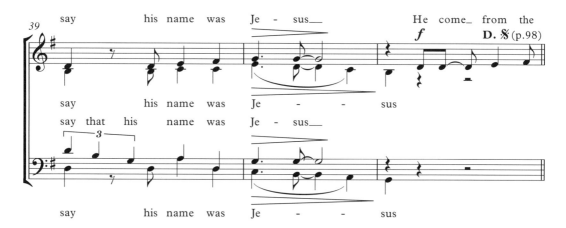

CODA

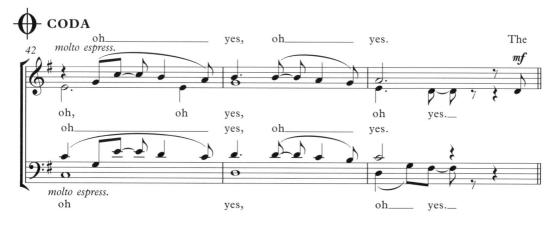

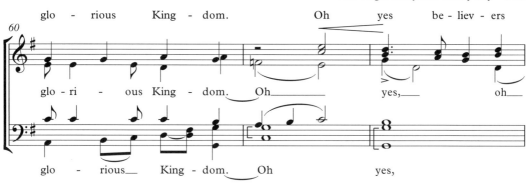

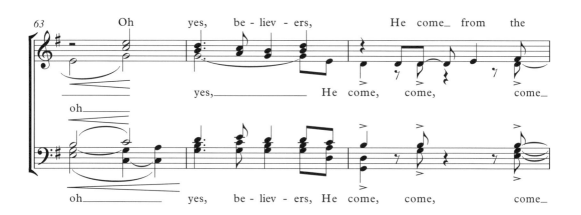

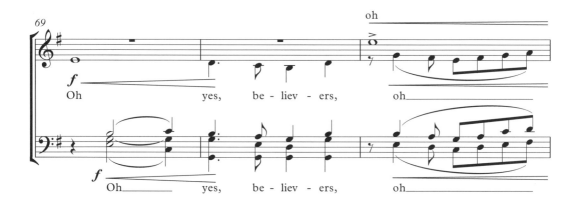

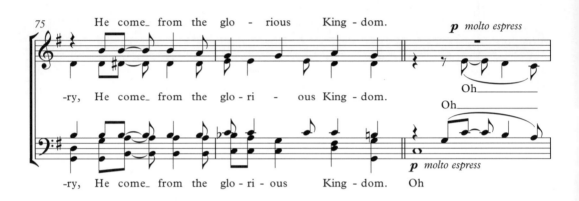

12. Wasn't that a mighty day!

arr. KEN BURTON

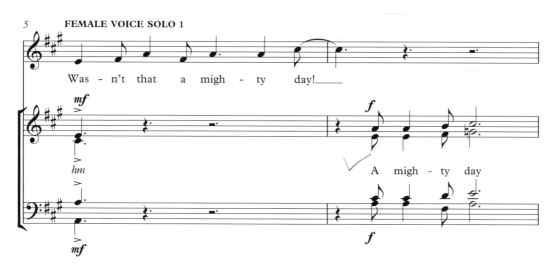

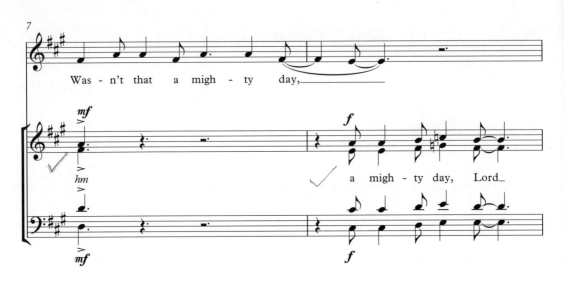

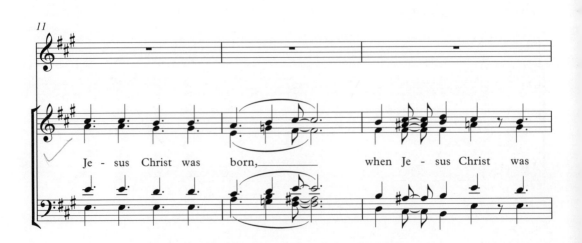